D0064972

THE SOLAR SYSTEM

URANUS

A MyReportLinks.com Book

GLENN SCHERER & MARTY FLETCHER

MyReportLinks.com Books

an imprint of

 Enslow Publishers, Inc.

Box 398, 40 Industrial Road
Berkeley Heights, NJ 07922
USA

MyReportLinks.com Books, an imprint of Enslow Publishers, Inc. MyReportLinks®
is a registered trademark of Enslow Publishers, Inc.

Library of Congress Cataloging-in-Publication Data

Scherer, Glen.
  Uranus / Glen Scherer & Marty Fletcher.
     p. cm. — (The solar system)
  Includes bibliographical references and index.
  ISBN 0-7660-5307-5
  1. Uranus (Planet)—Juvenile literature. I. Fletcher, Marty. II. Title. III. Solar system (Berkeley Heights, N.J.)
  QB681.S34 2005
  523.47—dc22
                                    2004012126

Printed in the United States of America

10 9 8 7 6 5 4 3 2 1

To Our Readers:
Through the purchase of this book, you and your library gain access to the Report Links that specifically back up this book.

The Publisher will provide access to the Report Links that back up this book and will keep these Report Links up to date on **www.myreportlinks.com** for five years from the book's first publication date.

We have done our best to make sure all Internet addresses in this book were active and appropriate when we went to press. However, the author and the Publisher have no control over, and assume no liability for, the material available on those Internet sites or on other Web sites they may link to.

The usage of the MyReportLinks.com Books Web site is subject to the terms and conditions stated on the Usage Policy Statement on **www.myreportlinks.com**.

A password may be required to access the Report Links that back up this book. The password is found on the bottom of page 4 of this book.

Any comments or suggestions can be sent by e-mail to comments@myreportlinks.com or to the address on the back cover.

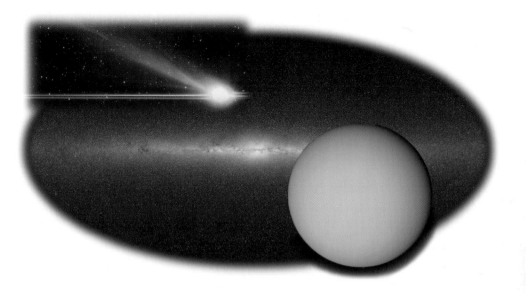

MyReportLinks.com Books
Great Books, Great Links, Great for Research!

The Internet sites listed on the next four pages can save you hours of research time. These Internet sites—we call them "Report Links"—are constantly changing, but we keep them up to date on our Web site.

Give it a try! Type http://www.myreportlinks.com into your browser, click on the series title, then the book title, and scroll down to the Report Links listed for this book.

The Report Links will bring you to great source documents, photographs, and illustrations. MyReportLinks.com Books save you time, feature Report Links that are kept up to date, and make report writing easier than ever!

Please see "To Our Readers" on the copyright page for important information about this book, the MyReportLinks.com Web site, and the Report Links that back up this book.

Please enter **PUR1445** if asked for a password.

> ## The Internet sites described below can be accessed at http://www.myreportlinks.com

*EDITOR'S CHOICE

▶Windows to the Universe: Uranus
Made up mostly of methane ice, the interior of Uranus helps to generate heat that creates the unusual wind patterns the planet is known for. This site provides information on the Voyager mission and the planet's atmosphere, rings, and moons.

*EDITOR'S CHOICE

▶The Nine Planets: Uranus
Discovered by William Herschel in 1781, Uranus is the third largest planet in our solar system. At this site, you will find a good overview of Uranus and detailed information on its satellites.

*EDITOR'S CHOICE

▶Images of Uranus
This NASA site offers a collection of seventeen photographs of the planet Uranus. The images depict its atmosphere, clouds, rotation, moons, and rings.

*EDITOR'S CHOICE

▶Welcome to the Planets: Uranus
This site on Uranus includes information about Miranda, Uranus's small and very unusual moon. Its surface has rolling hills, mountainous ridges, cliffs, and cratered valleys.

*EDITOR'S CHOICE

▶Voyager: The Interstellar Mission
Flying past Uranus in January 1986, the *Voyager 2* space probe was able to send a large amount of scientific data and thousands of images back to Earth. This site describes the other discoveries made during the mission to Uranus and other planets.

*EDITOR'S CHOICE

▶Solar System Exploration: Uranus
Uranus is larger in diameter but smaller in mass than Neptune. With no solid surface, Uranus is categorized as one of the gas giants. This NASA site, with a photo gallery, is one of the best sites for information on the seventh planet.

Report Links

The Internet sites described below can be accessed at
http://www.myreportlinks.com

▶**About Uranus**

What is so special about Uranus? Read what a member of the Voyager mission team has to say about the planet on this NASA educational site. Make sure you click on the link at the end of the page for Part Two.

▶**Ask an Astronomer**

This Cornell University site is a great place to visit if you are looking for information on planets. You can also use the search engine to find material on Uranus or any other planet.

▶**Diamonds in the Sky**

Could Uranus and Neptune be raining diamonds? These gas giants have large amounts of hydrocarbons in their atmosphere, and diamonds are crystalline carbons. Find out more at this PBS site.

▶**Enigma of Uranus Solved at Last**

This article discusses findings by scientists from Harvard University who think they have figured out why Uranus's and Neptune's strange magnetic fields differ from those of the other planets.

▶**Exploring the Planets: Uranus**

The *Voyager 2* space probe has confirmed the existence of eleven Uranian rings. One of the planet's unique characteristics is that it rolls in its orbit and tilts. At this site, learn more about this dynamic world with the brightest clouds in the outer solar system.

▶**Faraway Mystery Planet Uranus**

Uranus is sometimes referred to as Herschel, after its discoverer. Many of its moons are named for Shakespearean characters such as Desdemona, Juliet, and Ophelia. Learn more about the moons and Voyager probe at this site.

▶**Field Guide to the Universe: Uranus**

This guide to Uranus comes from the Children's Museum of Indianapolis. At this site, you will find materials on the planet's discovery, composition, poles, moons, and more.

▶**Friedrich Wilhelm Herschel**

William Herschel discovered Uranus in 1781 while he systematically searched the sky with a telescope he made himself. He also discovered two of its moons. This site offers a biography of the important eighteenth-century astronomer.

The Internet sites described below can be accessed at http://www.myreportlinks.com

▶HubbleSite

The Hubble Space Telescope is a reflecting telescope the size of a school bus. The most sophisticated space telescope now in orbit, it has given us important images of Uranus. Read more about the Hubble at this site.

▶*A Meeting With the Universe*

Written by NASA scientists for nonscientists, *A Meeting With the Universe* is available in full text on this site. Find out what astronauts have to say about the American space program.

▶National Maritime Museum: Uranus

This site from Britain's National Maritime Museum includes an article about Uranus that includes some interesting facts about the seventh planet.

▶The National Space Science Data Center: Uranus

This NASA resource page for Uranus includes information and statistics on the planet's satellites, atmosphere, orbital patterns, and rings. You will also find an image gallery.

▶Sagan Planet Walk: Uranus

The Sagan Planet Walk is a scale-model of the solar system in Ithaca, New York, built as a memorial to Cornell University's famous astronomer Carl Sagan. Visit the Uranus monument at this site.

▶StarDate Online: Uranus

Uranus spins sideways and has twenty-seven known moons. This site provides a good description of Uranus. Follow the links on the right-hand side for more information.

▶The Surface Temperatures of the Planets

You will learn which factors affect the surface temperatures of planets from Britain's National Maritime Museum site. The Sun plays a factor, as does a planet's magnetic field and core.

▶A Tour of the Solar System: Uranus

Information on Uranus, including its discovery, unusual magnetic poles, atmosphere, and moons is included in this site.

Report Links

The Internet sites described below can be accessed at
http://www.myreportlinks.com

▶ Tour the Solar System and Beyond: Uranus

The third largest planet in our solar system, Uranus is cataloged as a gas giant because it has no solid surface. Learn more about Uranus and its extreme seasons from this NASA site for kids.

▶ The Uranian Ring System

The rings of Uranus were discovered in 1977 when a star passed behind Uranus, and scientists aboard NASA's Kuiper Airborne Observatory noticed starlight winking on and off as the star approached the planet. Learn more about the planet's rings from this site.

▶ Uranus

Learn about Uranus from this fun BBC site, which is written from the perspective of a traveler to the planet. Information about how long it takes to get there and what you will see when you get there is included.

▶ Views of the Solar System: Uranus

Learn about Uranus from this site. Information on the planet's atmosphere, rings, and moons is included. A table with interesting statistics and some photographs are also available.

▶ Voyager: Mission to the Outer Planets

This National Air and Space Museum Web site describes Voyager, a two-spacecraft mission to Jupiter, Saturn, Uranus, and Neptune. Read about the Voyager components and instrumentation, and find out about the interesting things on board the probes.

▶ Voyager Gallery of Uranus's Ring System

In 1977, the first nine rings of Uranus were discovered and photographed by Voyager. They are much different from the rings of Jupiter and Saturn. Click on the images to get larger versions and additional information.

▶ The William Herschel Museum

William Herschel and his sister Caroline made up one of the most important teams in the history of astronomy. This museum site explains how the Herschels happened to discover Uranus.

▶ William Herschel's Catalog of Deep Sky Objects

This site takes a look at the life of William Herschel, the astronomer who discovered Uranus and went on to catalog more than 2,500 space discoveries. His sister's collaboration and the best telescope of the time helped him with these discoveries.

Uranus Facts

Age
About 4.5 billion years

Diameter
31,800 miles (51,200 kilometers)

Composition
Thick atmosphere mostly of hydrogen and helium, plus methane. Core is mostly rock surrounded by watery mud.

Average Distance From the Sun
About 1.8 million miles (3 billion kilometers)

Closest Approach to Earth
1.6 billion miles (2.5 billion kilometers)

Orbital Period (year, in Earth years)
About 84 Earth years

Rotational Period (day, in Earth hours)
17.2 Earth hours (17 hours 14 minutes)

Mass
About 15 times Earth's mass

Average Temperature
−350°F (−212°C) at cloud tops

Number of Moons
Twenty-seven

Number of Rings
Eleven

Largest Moon
Titania, 1,000 miles (1,600 kilometers) in diameter

Surface Gravity
91 percent of Earth's gravity

—	🏃	🏃	🛑 STOP	📖	🏠	🔑	▯	⌛
	Back	Forward	Stop	Review	Home	Explore	Favorites	History

Chapter 1 ▶

A Great Discovery

On the night of March 13, 1781, an English musician and amateur astronomer named William Herschel looked at the starry sky through his small homebuilt telescope. While peering at the constellation of Gemini, the Twins, he made an astounding discovery. At first, he did not know what he had found. He made an entry in his journal: Herschel noted "a curious either Nebulous

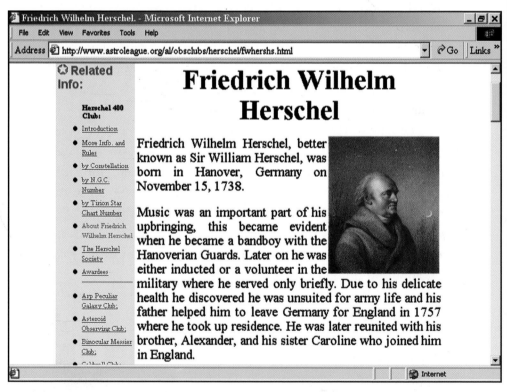

🔺 *William Herschel, who was born in Germany but moved to England, was an amateur astronomer who became one of the most famous astronomers of the eighteenth century with his discovery of Uranus.*

Star or perhaps a Comet."[1] (*Nebulous* is an astronomical term for a fuzzy, cloudlike object.)

More telescopic observations of the object revealed its slow movement against a background of changeless stars. That caused Herschel to change his opinion about the "nebulous star." He and his sister, Caroline Herschel, also an amateur astronomer, became convinced that this object was a planet that had never been identified. Other astronomers soon confirmed that belief. What they saw, which was just barely visible to the naked eye, was a tiny, fuzzy, blue disk when seen later through Herschel's most powerful telescope. It was the first new planet in our solar system to be discovered in modern history.

Since the dawn of time, ancient stargazers had watched the motions of the known celestial bodies. They had marveled at the Sun and Moon and at other bright "wandering" points of light that moved among the fixed stars of the constellations. The word *planet* means "wanderer" in Latin. The ancient Romans named these known planet-wanderers for their greatest gods—Mercury, Venus, Mars, Jupiter, and Saturn.

The new world discovered by Herschel excited scientists and the general public. It was soon identified as the farthest planet from the Sun at that time. It was an incredibly distant globe that orbited through depths of cold and dark space. It was calculated to be 1.8 billion miles (3 billion kilometers) from the Sun. That is a distance so great that if you could drive there in a fast car, going 60 miles per hour (97 kilometers per hour), it would take you about 30 million years to get there.

Naming the Planet

Since Herschel had discovered the planet, he believed that he had the right to name it. He decided to call it George, which seems an odd name for a planet. But he had named it in honor of King George III, then the king of England. In Latin, the name was *Georgium Sidus,* or Georgian Star. Although Herschel had been

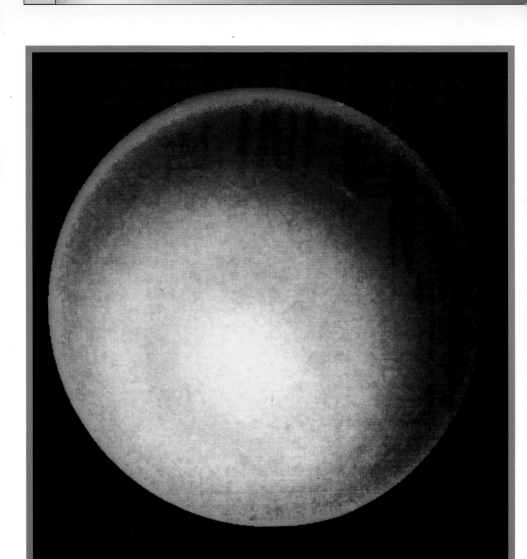

▲ A computer-enhanced image taken by Voyager 2 emphasizes the hazy atmosphere of Uranus, which hides the planet's clouds.

born in Germany in 1738, his family had moved to England in 1757. But astronomers from around the world complained that the new planet should not be named for a British king or for Herschel himself, a British subject. German astronomer Johann Bode suggested that the new planet be named, like the other known planets, after a mythological god. He proposed *Uranus,* the most ancient father of the Roman gods and the god of the sky and the heavens. It was a name that made sense: In Roman mythology, Jupiter was the father of Mars, Saturn the father of Jupiter, and Uranus the father of Saturn. The name stuck.

▷ Instant Fame

The discovery of this new world changed William and Caroline Herschel's lives forever. William had been a church organist and Caroline a soloist in a choir. But after the discovery of Uranus, King George III appointed William Herschel the court astronomer and gave a yearly salary to both William and Caroline. From then on, brother and sister put all their energy into astronomy, becoming two of the most famous scientists of the eighteenth century. Working as a team, they made the first telescopic survey of the sky. Caroline, the first woman to be recognized as an astronomer, discovered eight new comets.

The discovery of the planet Uranus also changed the future of astronomy, creating new interest in an old science. The discovery inspired young amateur astronomers, planet hunters, and comet hunters. To this day, stargazers turn their telescopes toward the sky and add new discoveries to our knowledge of the solar system.

▷ Secrets Recently Revealed

As for Uranus, its great distance from Earth kept most of its secrets from being revealed until late in the twentieth century. In 1986, a space probe named *Voyager 2* made the first flyby of Uranus. With its immense atmospheric pressure, Uranus would crush any spacecraft that tried to reach the planet's surface. *Voyager 2* had been launched nine years earlier by the National Aeronautics and Space Administration, or NASA. At its closest, *Voyager 2* came within 50,600 miles (81,415 kilometers) of Uranus's clouds. But it was able to transmit back to Earth thousands of images and a great deal of data about the planet.

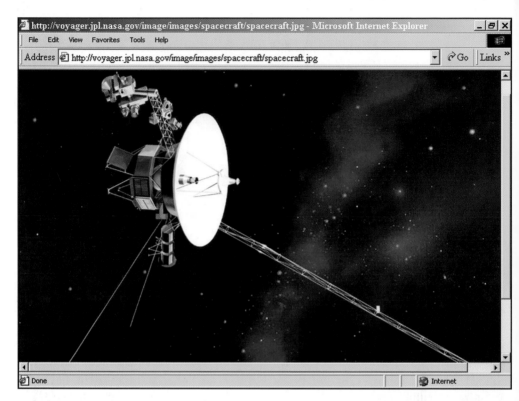

▲ The Voyager 2 *space probe came within 50,600 miles of Uranus in 1986—close enough to transmit thousands of never-before-seen images of the seventh planet from the Sun.*

The *Voyager 2* space probe and the Hubble Space Telescope have dramatically filled in our knowledge of Uranus. We have learned that Uranus is a very active planet and a super-cold and windy world. We are not yet able to land on it—its stormy atmosphere would be poisonous and deadly to any astronaut who tried to breathe it.

The Anatomy of a Gas Giant

For 205 years after its discovery, Uranus frustrated astronomers who pointed their telescopes at the planet. From so far away, it seemed a bland world. It looked like a featureless, faint blue disk where not much interesting ever happened. Scientists were able to calculate the planet's orbit and size and count a couple of its moons.

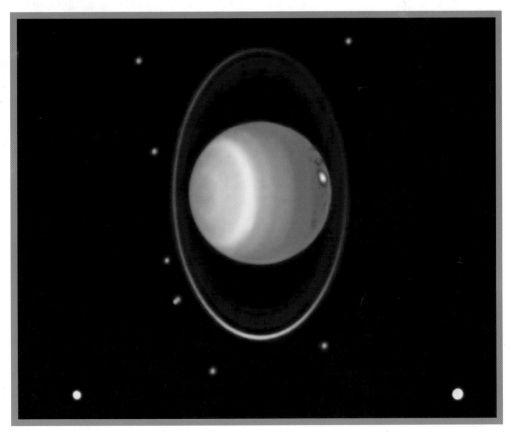

▲ This view of Uranus using images taken by the Hubble Space Telescope has been colorized to enhance its four major rings and some of its moons.

But they were still not sure what its atmosphere was like. And they did not know whether a rocky surface lay hidden somewhere far below the dense blue clouds.

Scientists did recognize Uranus as being one of four great gas giants in our solar system. These four outer planets—Jupiter, Saturn, Uranus, and Neptune—are many times larger than the four small, rocky planets closest to the Sun—Mercury, Venus, Earth, and Mars. The four outer planets are called gas giants because they are blanketed in thick atmospheres that are made up of a mixture of gases. Some planetary scientists now prefer to call Uranus and Neptune "ice giants."

The Storm Clouds of Uranus

Most of the thick atmosphere on Uranus—about 98 percent of it—is composed of the two simplest gases: 83 percent of the atmosphere is made of hydrogen, and 15 percent is made of helium. From a distance, Uranus reflects bright blue, but it only takes on that color because of small amounts of another gas in the atmospheric mix. About 2 percent of the total atmosphere is super-cold methane that condenses in the upper atmosphere to form clouds of methane ice crystals. These ice crystals absorb all of the red and yellow sunlight that reaches Uranus and only reflect back a bluish color to our eyes and instruments. The atmosphere also contains trace amounts of ammonia and other gases.

Temperatures on Uranus's cloud tops are extremely cold. They stay at an average of −350°F (−212°C). Many scientists expected there to be little energy for storms to occur in such a frigid place. But in 1999, the Hubble Space Telescope was pointed at Uranus. To everyone's surprise, violent storms were spotted. Some of these wild storms covered vast areas over a thousand miles wide. If a similar storm were to happen on Earth, it would stretch from New York to Kansas.

These violent storms on Uranus were happening as spring occurred in the northern part of the planet. "No one had ever

The thick atmosphere of  *Uranus is made up mostly of hydrogen and helium, with some methane. It is methane that gives the planet its bluish appearance.*

seen this view in the modern era of astronomy because of the long year of Uranus—more than 84 Earth years," said Dr. Heidi Hammel of the Massachusetts Institute of Technology.[1]

The Hubble Space Telescope also allowed scientists to discover that clouds on Uranus were being pushed along at speeds of more than 310 miles per hour (500 kilometers per hour). The only times on Earth that winds exceed that speed are during the most violent tornadoes. So Uranus, a planet that seemed pretty tame and uninteresting to astronomers, turned out to have much more exciting weather than they imagined.

The Mysterious Surface of Uranus

Not surprisingly, little is known about what lies far below the thick clouds of Uranus. Before *Voyager 2* flew by the planet in 1986, scientists guessed that a hot, rocky core about the size of Earth might lay hidden under the vast blanket of clouds. They thought they could detect this rocky core because of the gravitational tug it seemed to put on the planet's moons.

They also guessed that an extremely dense layer of water, ammonia, and methane covered this hot, rocky core, and on top of it was a thick layer of liquid hydrogen that merged with the atmosphere. This hydrogen would be under incredible pressure from the weight of the entire atmosphere pressing down on it. The pressure would be so great that the hydrogen—a gas here on Earth—would behave more like a runny liquid-metal on Uranus. But scientists now know that Uranus does not have enough gravity to compress hydrogen to a metallic state.

While these were all good theories, they turned out to be mostly wrong. As scientists learned more from *Voyager 2*'s instruments, they gave up their old theory about a liquid hydrogen "ocean" and developed a new theory. By the late 1980s, they became convinced that the atmosphere of Uranus goes all the way down to a layer of watery mud. This layer surrounds a core that is between ten and fifteen times the size of Earth.

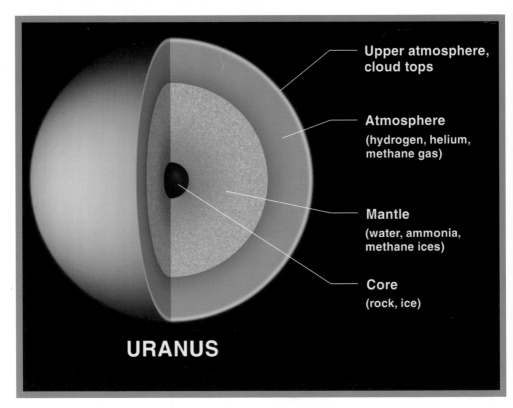

Upper atmosphere, cloud tops

Atmosphere
(hydrogen, helium, methane gas)

Mantle
(water, ammonia, methane ices)

Core
(rock, ice)

URANUS

▲ *A cutaway diagram shows the layers of Uranus. Scientists who study the planet believe its core is made mostly of ice and rock.*

Uranus
Hubble Space Telescope • WFPC2

PRC97-36b • November 20, 1997 • ST ScI OPO • H. Hammel (Massachusetts Institute of Technology) and NASA

▲ *Color has been added to these images of Uranus taken by the Hubble Space Telescope to show what someone on a spacecraft near the planet might see.*

Even with this new knowledge, astronomers still have much to learn about the atmosphere of Uranus. They are continuing to search for what causes the planet's intense storms and very strong winds and to find out what minerals the rocky core might be made of.

Strange Days on Uranus

Its characteristics, including its peculiar orbit, rotation, and magnetic field, all make Uranus a planet unlike any other in our solar system. To begin with, it takes Uranus about eighty-four Earth years to orbit the Sun, which means that a year on Uranus is nearly a century on Earth. In the time it takes Uranus to orbit the Sun once, an entire human lifetime can slip by.

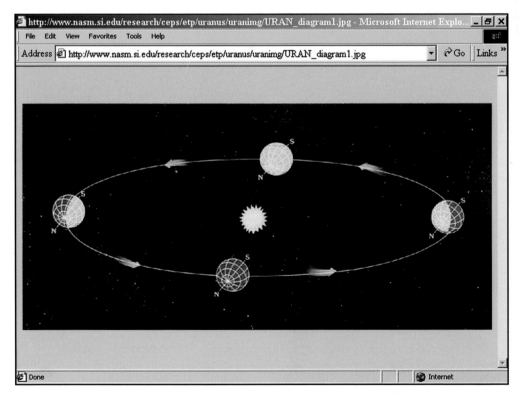

http://www.nasm.si.edu/research/ceps/etp/uranus/uranimg/URAN_diagram1.jpg - Microsoft Internet Explo...

File Edit View Favorites Tools Help

Address http://www.nasm.si.edu/research/ceps/etp/uranus/uranimg/URAN_diagram1.jpg

Done   Internet

▲ Uranus is tilted at such an angle that it tips on its side as it rotates on its axis. This tilt creates the planet's strange and long seasons: Uranus is pointed toward the Sun and then away from the Sun for forty-two Earth years at a time.

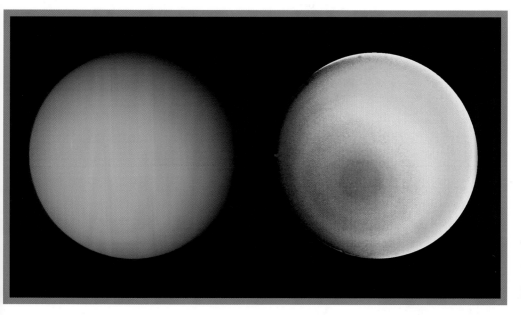

▲ These Voyager 2 *images of Uranus look toward the planet's pole of rotation. The image of Uranus on the left has been processed to show the planet as humans would see it from a spacecraft, while the image on the right uses false color to highlight the polar haze.*

▷ Long Days, Long Seasons

It takes Uranus just a little over 17 hours to complete one rotation on its axis, as compared to Earth's 24-hour rotation, which we call a day. But a "day" on Uranus would not *feel* 17 hours long—it would feel much longer, 84 years long.

The reason for this is the planet's tilt: As Uranus rotates on its axis, it is tipped on its side. All the other planets in our solar system spin mostly upright like tops, but Uranus rolls along sidewise, parallel to its orbit. Its tilt means that one side of the planet is pointed toward the Sun for forty-two years at a time, while the other side sits in total darkness. Seasons and daylight drag on for decades.

The tilt of Uranus's axis is the reason that its north and south poles are sometimes pointed directly at the Sun. The planet's south pole faced almost directly toward the Sun during most of the 1990s. If during that decade you had stood somewhere in the southern hemisphere of Uranus and looked up through its atmosphere (something that is impossible to do), you would have seen the tiny dot of the Sun almost straight overhead. It would be turning very tiny circles in the sky every 17.2 hours as the planet rotated. But the Sun would not have risen or set during those years. The polar regions of Uranus go through four seasons, just as we have four seasons on Earth, but seasons on Uranus last much longer. There is total sunlight in summer and total darkness in winter, and these seasons last for about twenty-one Earth years. It is only during spring and fall that there are alternating periods of daylight and nighttime on Uranus.

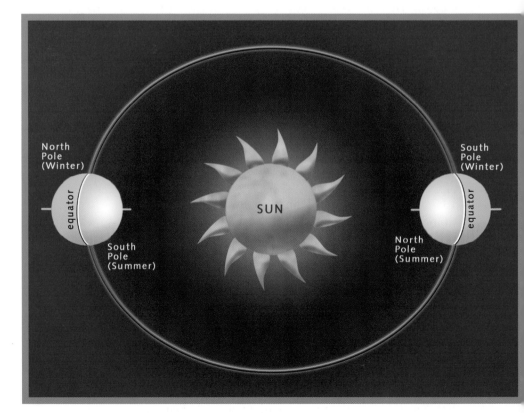

North
Pole
(Winter)

equator

South
Pole
(Summer)

SUN

South
Pole
(Winter)

equator

North
Pole
(Summer)

▲ *Uranus rotates on its side as it revolves around the Sun, which means that there is complete darkness on Uranus's north pole when its south pole faces the sun.*

With such long seasons, it would seem likely that temperatures on Uranus would vary widely from winter to summer. But because Uranus is so far from the Sun, even when the Sun is shining straight overhead, the planet heats up very little. Temperatures on Uranus's cloud tops are about the same no matter what the season: a frosty −350°F (−212°C). That is cold enough to turn gases like methane into ice.

In 1999, the northern latitudes of Uranus began to peek out of darkness and point toward the Sun. By the 2030s, its north pole will face the Sun and Earth while its south pole is in the dark. By the 2070s, the south pole of Uranus will again be point-ing directly at the Sun.[1]

Why does Uranus rotate on its side? One interesting theory suggests that a catastrophic collision with a planet or asteroid knocked Uranus's axis on its side. This collision, much like a marble hitting another marble at high speed, drastically changed the way the planet spins. Miranda, one of the moons that orbits Uranus, supports that theory: It appears to have been blown apart and reassembled! Some scientists think that such a disaster could only have happened to Miranda when Uranus was struck by another planet.

The Magnetic Field of Uranus

Voyager 2 also discovered a strong magnetic field surrounding Uranus. Such intense magnetic fields have also been found around Saturn and Jupiter.

Uranus's magnetic field is about one hundred times stronger than Earth's, though its strength seems to vary from place to place around Uranus. Scientists are not sure of the source of Uranus's magnetic field, but they think that high pressure on the planet ionizes, or charges, certain compounds, so that water that is pres-ent becomes a good conductor of electricity. Scientists have seen that the planet's magnetic field creates brilliant auroras in the planet's magnetic polar regions, similar to the northern and

This photograph captures the aurora borealis, or northern lights, above Grand Junction, Colorado. Scientists have observed brilliant auroras like this on Uranus.

southern lights on Earth with their ghostly display of sky colors.[2] Auroras are caused by charged atomic particles that glow high in the upper atmosphere. The planet's magnetic axis, like its rotational axis, is also tipped so that these axes are tilted away from each other.

Uranus is surrounded by an intense radiation belt that reaches far into space. This belt is made up of electrons and protons that have become trapped by the planet's strong magnetic field. These particles speed about and collide, generating radio waves. As *Voyager 2* approached the planet, these charged particles "sang" to the spacecraft, causing a wild and harsh "sound" of radio waves that were recorded by the probe's instruments. Like the other gas giants, Uranus has a vast magnetic tail that extends for millions of miles behind the planet. *Voyager 2* measured this "magnetotail" and found that it trailed at least 6.2 million miles (10 million kilometers) behind the planet.

The Rings and Moons of Uranus

While the surface of Uranus remains hidden from us by thick clouds, its moons and rings were revealed in all their beauty to *Voyager 2* on its close approach to Uranus in 1986. With Uranus tipped on its side, its moons and rings could be seen as what NASA called "a giant celestial bull's eye."[1]

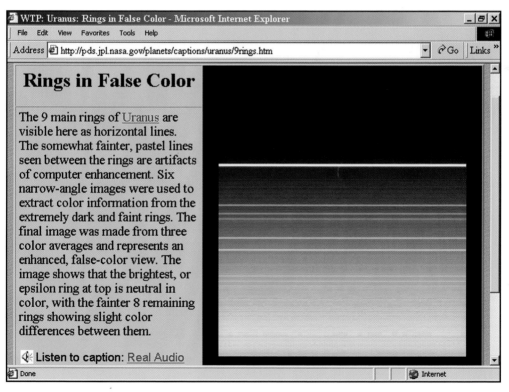

WTP: Uranus: Rings in False Color - Microsoft Internet Explorer

File   Edit   View   Favorites   Tools   Help

Address http://pds.jpl.nasa.gov/planets/captions/uranus/9rings.htm   Go   Links

Rings in False Color

The 9 main rings of Uranus are visible here as horizontal lines. The somewhat fainter, pastel lines seen between the rings are artifacts of computer enhancement. Six narrow-angle images were used to extract color information from the extremely dark and faint rings. The final image was made from three color averages and represents an enhanced, false-color view. The image shows that the brightest, or epsilon ring at top is neutral in color, with the fainter 8 remaining rings showing slight color differences between them.

◀ **Listen to caption:** Real Audio

Done   Internet

△ Color has been added to this photograph of the nine main rings of Uranus taken by Voyager 2 in 1986. The fainter lines in between the nine darker ones are the result of computer enhancement. The first nine rings of the planet's ring system were discovered fewer than thirty years ago.

Spending just six hours near the planet, *Voyager 2* was like a frantic tourist on vacation who hurriedly snaps pictures of all there is to see. In the spacecraft's brief visit, it took thousands of photos and greatly expanded our knowledge of the moons and rings of Uranus. Scientists continue to study the photos and instrument readings from the space probe and to learn more from them. The Hubble Space Telescope, which orbits Earth, has also added much to what we know about the rings and moons of Uranus.

The Rings of Uranus

In 1977, a group of astronomers, led by James Elliot of the Massachusetts Institute of Technology, flew a large plane above the Indian Ocean and made an exciting discovery.

The aircraft, known as the Kuiper Airborne Observatory, was loaded with telescopes and other instruments. It was flying in that part of the world to observe a rare event: Uranus was passing in front of a star.

What the scientists found was that just before the star went behind Uranus, it winked a few times. Then, as the star came back out from behind Uranus, the star winked rhythmically a few more times. These "winkings" on and off of the star meant that something near Uranus was blocking out the starlight.

The scientists were not sure what was blocking the starlight, but they soon figured out that this mysterious "something" was a planetary ring system.

The outermost ring of Uranus, which is the most prominent in this photograph, is called Epsilon. The next three, fainter rings, are Delta, Gamma, and Eta. All are named for letters of the Greek alphabet.

These nine rings of Uranus were the first to be found in the solar system since 1610, when the astronomer Galileo first saw the rings of Saturn through his small telescope. In 1979, *Voyager 1* discovered rings around Jupiter, and in 1989, *Voyager 2* proved that there is a complete ring system around Neptune.

On *Voyager 2*'s visit to Uranus in 1986, its rings were photographed close up, and two more rings were discovered. The eleven rings counted by *Voyager* are thought to be composed of billions of tiny pebbles, varying in size from a few inches across to as much as 33 feet (10 meters) in diameter. Unlike the shiny rings of Saturn, the rings of Uranus were almost black.

▷ Wobbling Pebbles

Scientists found something else surprising about Uranus's rings: They do not spin smoothly around the planet as the ring systems of other gas giants do. Instead they wobble like an unbalanced wheel. This wobble may be caused by Uranus's shape, which is not spherical or oval but is a slightly flattened globe, or it may be caused by the gravitational pull of the many orbiting moons of Uranus.

The innermost ring spins just 7,700 miles (12,400 kilometers) above the cloud tops of Uranus. The outermost ring extends out from the planet about 16,000 miles (26,000 kilometers). Most of the eleven rings of Uranus are no larger than 6 miles (10 kilometers) wide, though the outermost ring is 62 miles (100 kilometers) from inside to outside.

The ring system of Uranus, like the planetary ring systems of Saturn, Jupiter, and Neptune, is very thin compared to its immense width. The rings of Uranus are only about 33 to 330 feet (10 to 100 meters) thick.[2]

The rings of Uranus also change. Besides wobbling, the ring's rocky particles are constantly being lost and replaced by other particles. The outermost ring's space debris is kept from drifting away from the planet by the gravitational effect of two of Uranus's moons, Cordelia and Ophelia, which orbit close to the planet.

The Many Moons of Uranus

As of 2004, scientists believe Uranus has twenty-seven moons, although not all of the planet's moons have been named yet. Many of the moons—such as Puck, Juliet, and Prospero—are named after characters in the plays of the great English playwright William Shakespeare and those from poems of the English poet Alexander Pope.

The five largest moons of Uranus were discovered by Earthbound telescopes before 1950. Ten small, very dark inner moons were found by *Voyager 2* in 1986. Since the 1980s, the rest have been found by the Hubble Space Telescope as well as by large and powerful Earthbound telescopes.

A Look at the Biggest Moons

The five largest moons of Uranus range in size from about 300 miles (500 kilometers) to about 1,000 miles (1,600 kilometers) in diameter. They are all about half water ice and

This montage shows the five largest moons of Uranus, in order of decreasing distance from the planet: Oberon, Titania, Umbriel, Ariel, and Miranda.

Titania, the largest moon of Uranus, bears ▷ *scars from some kind of impact and has features that resemble trenches, indications of geologic activity.*

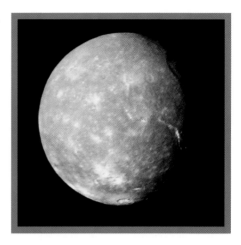

half rock, much like the moons of Saturn. Most of the moons of Uranus have craters while others are crisscrossed by valleys.

Titania, named for a queen in Shakespeare's play *A Midsummer Night's Dream,* is the largest moon of Uranus. It is 1,000 miles (1,609 kilometers) in diameter, almost half the size of Earth's Moon. Titania's surface is marked by craters, though some of them appear to be partially filled in with rock or ice or a combination of the two. Titania is also crisscrossed by larger faults and canyons, like interconnected valleys, and some of these are over 1,000 miles (1,609 kilometers) long and as much as 3 miles (5 kilometers) deep. These surface features are thought to be young in geologic terms. One theory about how Titania's valleys were created is that Titania was once so hot that it was liquid. The outer crust of the moon cooled first and then later, when the inner core froze, it expanded outward, cracking the surface. The valleys photographed by *Voyager 2* resulted.

Oberon, the second largest moon at 960 miles (1,550 kilometers) in diameter, is named for the king of the fairies, Titania's husband, in *A Midsummer Night's Dream.* Unlike Titania, Oberon has a surface that is heavily pockmarked by ancient craters. Some measure more than 60 miles (100 kilometers) across. One mountain on Oberon is at least 12 miles (20 kilometers) high, more than twice the height of Mount Everest, the highest mountain on Earth. The many ancient craters of Oberon, not filled in by any kind of material, make scientists think that this moon's surface and interior have remained much the same throughout the

▲ *Ariel's southern hemisphere is shown through color filters to accentuate this moon's features, including craters, fault scarps, and valleys.*

moon's history. Large faults in Oberon's southern hemisphere do show, however, that there may have once been geologic activity on this moon.

Umbriel, the third largest moon on Uranus, is 740 miles (1,191 kilometers) across. Named for a character in an Alexander Pope poem, Umbriel is heavily and evenly cratered, which seems to indicate that there has been little or no geological activity since the moon was first formed. Scientists do not know why, but Umbriel is the darkest of the large Uranian moons, reflecting only half as much light as Ariel, the brightest of the planet's other big satellites.

Ariel, at 720 miles (1,160 kilometers) in diameter, is the fourth largest of the moons of Uranus. Something has wiped away almost all evidence of craters on Ariel. Its surface has been remolded with valleys hundreds of miles long and 10 to 20 miles (16 to 32 kilometers) deep. Geologists are unsure what caused these valleys and the violent resurfacing of the planet. Some think that it was caused by flows of a glacierlike mixture of ice and rock that then hardened.

Uranus's fifth largest moon, Miranda, may be the most interesting. When *Voyager 2* trained its cameras on the surface of Miranda, astronomers were amazed and perplexed by the images they saw.

▷ The Strange Case of Miranda

Little Miranda, just 300 miles (500 kilometers) in diameter, is one of the strangest moons in all of the solar system. It is one seventh the size of Earth's Moon.

Amazed by what he learned about Miranda, the famous astronomer and author Carl Sagan wrote, "Its surface is a tumult of fault valleys, parallel ridges, sheer cliffs, low mountains, impact craters, and frozen floods of once-molten surface material. This turmoiled landscape is unexpected for a small, cold, icy world so distant from the Sun."[3] Miranda's jumbled, topsy-turvy features have left planetary geologists wondering how such features came to be formed.

This little moon has remarkable landforms found nowhere else in the solar system. There is a single cliff more than 12 miles (19 kilometers) high. With Miranda's low gravity, if an astronaut fell from that cliff's top, it would take ten minutes before he or she hit the valley floor, even while accelerating all the way down! For such a towering cliff to exist on such a tiny moon makes no sense in terms of the way we know that mountains form. Miranda also features giant fault canyons that are twelve times as deep as Earth's Grand Canyon. Given the low temperatures found on Miranda, −335°F (−204°C), the tectonic activity, or shifting of large plates of land, on this moon is even more astonishing.

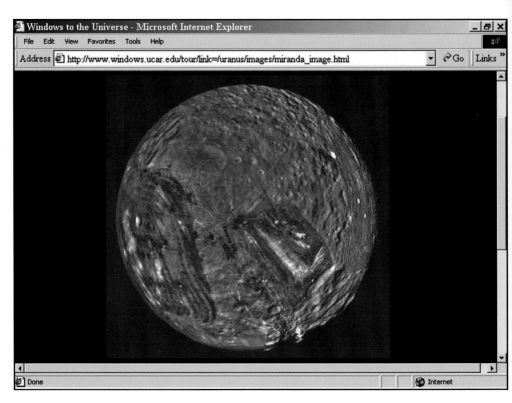

Windows to the Universe - Microsoft Internet Explorer

File   Edit   View   Favorites   Tools   Help

Address   http://www.windows.ucar.edu/tour/link=/uranus/images/miranda_image.html   Go   Links

Done   Internet

▲ Miranda, with towering cliffs and deep craters, is one of the strangest moons in our solar system.

Scientists have developed several theories to explain the strange features on Miranda. Some think that the gravitational influence of other close-by moons caused the interior of Miranda to melt and then erupt in huge volcanoes and earthquakes. Others think that Miranda may have been badly damaged by the same planet that might have collided with Uranus and knocked it off its axis long ago.

Still another theory is more dramatic. According to Carl Sagan, "Just conceivably, maybe Miranda was once utterly destroyed, dismembered, blasted into smithereens by a wild careening world, with many collision fragments still left in Miranda's orbit. The shards and remnants, slowly colliding, gravitationally attracting one another, may have reaggregated [reorganized] into just such a jumbled, patchy, unfinished world as Miranda is today."[4]

Could it be that Miranda is a moon that was exploded, destroyed, and then sewn back together by the force of gravity? It will probably take scientists many more years of study to unravel this mystery. A solution may only be found when a manned or unmanned probe orbits Uranus—or even lands on its tiny moon, Miranda.

The Smallest Moons of Uranus

All of the inner moons of Uranus discovered by *Voyager 2* are smaller than 62 miles (100 kilometers) across and are very close to the planet. Some of these inner moons have been given names from Shakespeare and Pope, but others are still unnamed, simply given

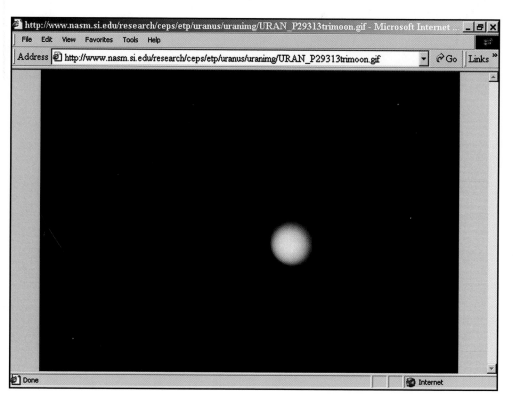

△ Uranus and three of its moons are captured in this image taken by Voyager 2.

A Hubble wide view of Uranus has been enhanced to reveal its faint rings and some of its moons.

a number corresponding to the year and order of discovery. The two tiniest moons, just 8 and 10 miles (13 and 16 kilometers) across, about the size of the city of San Francisco, were discovered in 2003.

"The inner swarm of 13 satellites is unlike any other system of planetary moons," says scientist Jack Lissauer. ". . . The region is so crowded that these moons could be gravitationally unstable."[5] That means they could, at any time, wander out of orbit or even collide. Some scientists feel sure that two of Uranus's tiny and yet-unnamed moons, S/2003 U2 and S/1986 U10, may have broken off from another nearby moon named Belinda. While some of the planet's innermost moons may have formed about the same time that Uranus formed and continue to orbit the planet, others may have been captured by the planet's gravitational field far more recently.

The most amazing thing about these small moons, known as moonlets, may be that scientists have been able to see them at all. "These moons are 40 million times fainter than Uranus," says scientist Mark Showalter. ". . . They are blacker than asphalt . . . so they don't reflect much light. Even with the sensitivity and high

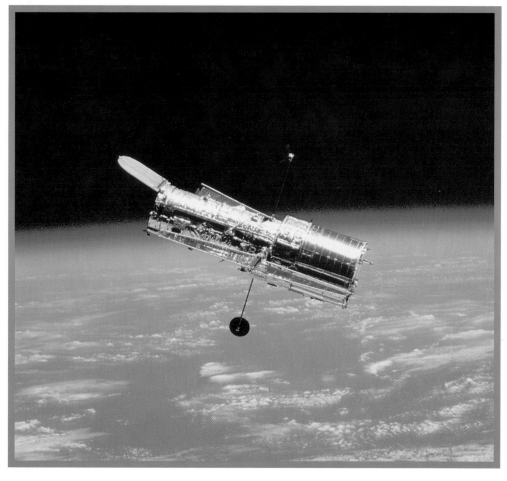

△ *The images captured by the Hubble Space Telescope have significantly increased our knowledge of Uranus.*

resolution of [the Hubble Space Telescope], we had to overexpose the images of Uranus to pinpoint the moons."[6] Astronomers are still trying to learn why these small moons, which orbit a crowded region, do not crash into each other. They believe that future investigations will find even more small moons orbiting Uranus, helping to keep the planet's ring systems in place.

		STOP						
Back	Forward	Stop	Review	Home	Explore	Favorites	History

Chapter 5 ▶

Uranus Explored

Many other astronomers saw Uranus and plotted it on their star maps before William Herschel discovered the planet late in the eighteenth century. But none of them recognized it as a planet. As far back as 1690, John Flamsteed, the British royal astronomer, sighted it. But he failed to observe it night after night and note its motion. He thought it was just another star.[1] It was not until nearly

▲ William Herschel used this telescope, which he designed and built, to discover the planet Uranus.

a century later that William Herschel, with a superior telescope and very careful continual plotting of star positions, was able to identify Uranus. Once he charted its movement against the background of fixed stars, he knew it was a new planet.

After Herschel's discovery of Uranus, astronomers continued watching the planet and making more discoveries about it. Herschel, who ground his own lenses and made some of the finest telescopes of the time, was able to spot two moons orbiting Uranus. In 1787, he discovered Titania and Oberon, the largest Uranian moons. Two more Uranian moons, Ariel and Umbriel, were found by William Lassell, a British brewer-turned-astronomer, in 1851. It was not until 1948 that the fifth of the largest moons of Uranus was spotted for the first time. Using an Earth-based telescope, the American astronomer Gerard Kuiper, considered the father of modern planetary astronomy, called the newfound moon Miranda.

Orbital Questions Lead to the Discovery of a New Planet

Astronomers were able to predict the orbit of Uranus as far back as the late 1700s. But no matter how carefully they made their mathematical calculations, Uranus continued to wander from its expected path. Scientists began to think that an unknown gravitational force was tugging on Uranus and changing its orbit and position. This led them to search for another planet beyond Uranus that would explain its unusual motion. It took three scientists from three nations to come up with the solution.

In the 1840s, Englishman John Couch Adams and Frenchman Urbain Le Verrier set out to use the "wandering" orbit of Uranus to calculate the position of the mystery planet. In 1846, using Le Verrier's calculations, a young German astronomer named Johann Galle pointed his nine-inch refracting telescope at the right part of the sky and discovered Neptune within hours of starting his search. Seventeen days later, Neptune's largest moon, Triton, was discovered.

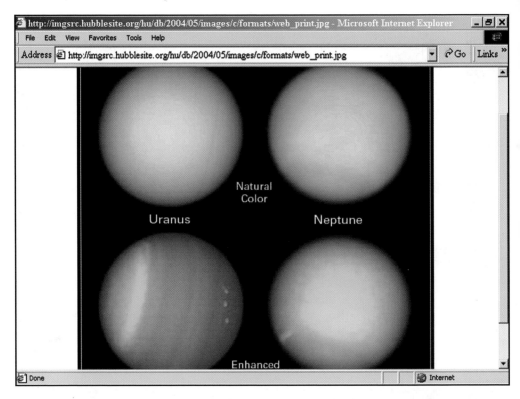

Natural
Color

Uranus   Neptune

Enhanced

▲ Hubble images of Uranus, left, and Neptune, right, compare the two gas giants. The top images show these planets, which appear similar, as we might see them through a telescope, while the bottom images reveal their differences: Uranus's rotational axis is tilted 90 degrees to Neptune's.

▷ The Voyager Space Probes

One of the greatest technological advances of modern times has been the invention of robotic space probes. They can travel to worlds where humans cannot, and they have given us mechanical eyes that allow us to see farther into the universe than any human eye has seen before.

NASA's two Voyager probes, launched in 1977, have journeyed farther and advanced our knowledge of the outer planets more than any other space probes. Engineers built the Voyager space probes in the mid-1970s, without the benefit of today's

△ *The Voyager missions were launched in 1977 to explore the outer planets of our solar system: Jupiter, Saturn, Neptune, and Uranus.* Voyager 2 *was actually launched sixteen days before* Voyager 1, *but their different paths caused* Voyager 1 *to arrive at Jupiter four months earlier.*

sophisticated computers, which makes their accomplishments even greater. When the Voyagers were launched, most computers were huge, taking up the entire space of a room. The very first compact personal computers had only just been invented. And by 1979, when the first popular but primitive computer video games, like Space Invaders and Pac-Man, were being created, the Voyager probes had already arrived near Jupiter.

Both tiny spacecraft hurtled through the depths of space at tens of thousands of miles per hour, and they traveled billions of miles to hit their targets perfectly, passing close by all four gas giants and their many moons. The two Voyager probes had been launched at a time when they could take advantage of a unique lineup of the planets. This lineup supplied enough gravitational force to "sling-shot" the space probes precisely from one fast orbiting world to the next. This "grand tour" of the planets sent *Voyager 1* to Saturn and Jupiter and then out of the solar system. *Voyager 2* also explored these two gas giants. Scientists then decided that the probe had performed so well that its mission should be extended to include a trip to Uranus and Neptune.

Voyager 2's Flyby

Voyager 2 took eight and a half years to complete its journey from Earth to Uranus. Though the space probe traveled through vast stretches of cold, empty space and was bombarded with solar radiation, *Voyager 2*'s instruments worked flawlessly.

On January 25, 1986, a little over two hundred years after Uranus was discovered, *Voyager 2* came within 50,600 miles (81,500 kilometers) of the planet. The probe had less than six hours to do its work before leaving Uranus forever. *Voyager 2* shot 4,300 pictures in that brief time. The NASA astronomers at the Jet Propulsion Laboratory in Pasadena, California, who were in control of the mission, cheered and applauded as the probe's photographs were beamed back to them across 1.75 billion miles (2.8 billion kilometers) of empty space. *Voyager 2* was so far away that each photo

▲ Voyager's "grand tour" of the outer planets is captured in this montage, which compares, from left to right, Neptune, Uranus, Saturn, and Jupiter.

took two and three-quarter hours to reach Earth, crossing the solar system at the speed of light.

As a bonus, *Voyager 2* flew within just 17,500 miles (28,158 kilometers) of Miranda, the strange little Uranian moon. Scientists watching the photos appear on their screens back home were thrilled with the shots, which showed Miranda's ragged ridges and slashed fractures looking like the scarred, battered face of an old boxer.

New Moons Discovered

Voyager 2 not only gave scientists the first close look at the five largest moons of Uranus, but it also revealed ten new ones, tripling the number of the planet's known moons. Most interesting of these was Puck, about 105 miles (170 kilometers) in diameter. All ten of these little moons appear to be very dark, almost tar colored. Scientists continue to debate why these moons are black, a debate that one scientist, Robert Hamilton Brown, has jokingly dubbed "tar wars."[2]

The Adventure Continues

After its encounter with Uranus, *Voyager 2* swept on to Neptune and the rest of the universe. The space probes are still sending remarkable data back to Earth, and they have enough operating power to continue to run until at least 2020. By then, *Voyager 1* will be 12.4 billion miles (19.9 billion kilometers) from the Sun, and *Voyager 2* will be 10.5 billion miles (16.9 billion kilometers) away from the Sun. Both Voyager probes are approaching the final boundary between the outermost reaches of our solar system and interstellar space (among the stars of our galaxy).

The scientists who pushed so hard to get the Voyager missions approved in the 1970s continue to be pleased by the results of these probes, which have proved to be far less expensive than one would think. If the total cost of the Voyager missions was divided among all Americans, each of us would have to pay just two dollars to finance the longest trip ever taken by spacecraft.

Hubble's Contributions

The Voyager probes are not the only vehicles that have helped us learn more about Uranus. The Hubble Space Telescope, about as large as a school bus, has added a great deal to our knowledge of the seventh planet. It orbits Earth at an altitude of 380 statute miles (611 kilometers) and a speed of 17,500 miles per hour (28,158 kilometers per hour), which allows it to travel around Earth in a little over an hour and a half.[3]

Images captured by the Hubble show spring happening in the northern hemisphere of Uranus and some of the fierce

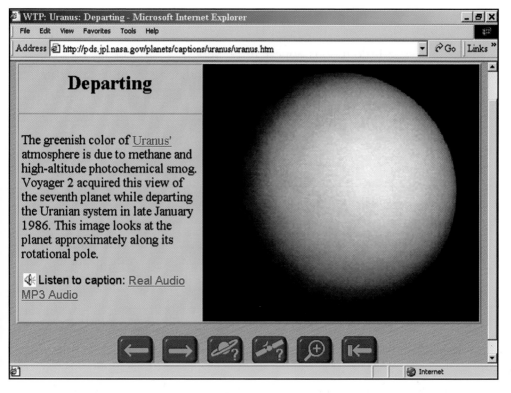

Departing

The greenish color of Uranus' atmosphere is due to methane and high-altitude photochemical smog. Voyager 2 acquired this view of the seventh planet while departing the Uranian system in late January 1986. This image looks at the planet approximately along its rotational pole.

🔊 **Listen to caption:** Real Audio
MP3 Audio

▲ *This parting shot of Uranus, looking at its rotational pole, was taken by Voyager 2 as it left Uranus in late January 1986. There is still much to learn about the planet.*

storms taking place on the planet. One of Hubble's greatest contributions has been the discovery of new Uranian moons, which with improved Earth-based telescopes, has brought the present known total to twenty-seven.

▷ Future Exploration of Uranus

While there are no plans under way at the moment to further explore Uranus, perhaps sometime in the next few decades, probes will be launched to Uranus. They may orbit it or dive into its thick atmosphere—or even land on its moons. There is no telling what wonders they might find.

▲ *This montage contains images of the solar system taken by the Voyager probes, with Earth's Moon in the foreground.* Voyager 2 *discovered Uranus's magnetic environment as well as ten of the planet's moons.*

Many decades in the future, humans may even set foot on those moons, carrying on the pioneering work of William Herschel and of *Voyager 2.* From Miranda or Oberon, those bold planetary explorers would look out on the huge blue ball of Uranus and look back at a tiny, pale blue dot that is our Earth.

Glossary

auroras—Bright bands of light seen in the northern and southern hemispheres of some planets.

electron—A particle with a negative electric charge that travels around the nucleus of an atom.

gas giants—Jupiter, Saturn, Neptune, and Uranus: The four large planets, mostly composed of gas, at the outer edge of our solar system.

Hubble Space Telescope—A telescope that orbits Earth about 400 miles (600 kilometers) above the planet's surface. Developed by the European Space Agency and NASA, the Hubble has identified ten more moons of Uranus.

magnetic axis—The imaginary line that joins the north and south poles of a planet's magnetic field. Uranus's magnetic axis is unusual in that it is tilted so much toward the planet's rotational axis.

magnetic field—A part of space near a magnetic body or a current-carrying body in which the magnetic forces can be detected.

planetary ring system—Material that has come together into thin, flat rings that circle the larger planets.

proton—A particle in the nucleus of an atom that carries a single positive electric charge.

rotational axis—The axis, or point, around which a planet or other body rotates.

satellite—A heavenly body, such as a moon, that orbits a larger body.

space probe—An unpiloted spacecraft used to make observations and send back data from space. The Voyager space probes have provided a great deal of what we know about Uranus.

Chapter 1. A Great Discovery

1. Michael Hoskin, *The Cambridge Illustrated History of Astronomy* (Cambridge: Cambridge University Press, 1997), p. 187.

Chapter 2. The Anatomy of a Gas Giant

1. Science @ NASA, Press Release, "Huge Storms Hit the Planet Uranus," March 9, 1999, <http://science.nasa.gov/newhome/headlines/ast29mar99_1.htm> (September 25, 2004).

Chapter 3. Strange Days on Uranus

1. Carl Sagan, *Pale Blue Dot* (New York: Random House, 1994), p. 128.

2. Mark Littman, *Planets Beyond* (New York: Wiley Science Editions, 1990), p. 118.

Chapter 4. The Rings and Moons of Uranus

1. NASA Jet Propulsion Laboratory, California Institute of Technology, "Before Voyager," January 14, 2003, <http://voyager.jpl.nasa.gov/science/uranus_before.html> (September 25, 2004).

2. Thomas R. Watters, *Smithsonian Guides: Planets* (New York: Simon and Schuster, 1995), p. 165.

3. Carl Sagan, *Pale Blue Dot* (New York: Random House, 1994), p. 131.

4. Ibid., p. 131.

5. Space Telescope Science Institute, Press Release, *Hubblesite,* "Hubble Uncovers Smallest Moons Yet Seen Around Uranus," September 25, 2003, <http://hubblesite.org/newscenter/newsdesk/archive/releases/2003/29/text/> (September 25, 2004).

6. Ibid.

Chapter 5. Uranus Explored

1. Mark Littman, *Planets Beyond* (New York: Wiley Science Editions, 1990), p. 24.

2. Ibid., p. 137.

3. NASA, Solar System Exploration, "Hubble Space Telescope," n.d., <http://solarsystem.nasa.gov/missions/profile.cfm?Sort=Planet&Object=Beyond&Mission=HST> (September 24, 2004).

Asimov, Isaac, with revisions and updating by Richard Hantula. *Uranus.* Milwaukee: Gareth Stevens Publishing, 2002.

Byman, Jeremy. *Carl Sagan: In Contact With the Cosmos.* Greensboro, N.C.: Morgan Reynolds, 2001.

Cole, Michael C. *Uranus—The Seventh Planet.* Berkeley Heights, N.J.: Enslow Publishers, Inc., 2002.

Farndon, John. *Planets and Their Moons.* Brookfield, Conn.: Copper Beech Books, 2001.

Garlick, Mark A. *Story of the Solar System.* Cambridge: Cambridge University Press, 2002.

Gutsche, William A. *1001 Things Everyone Should Know About the Universe.* New York: Doubleday, 1998.

Kerrod, Robin. *Hubble: The Mirror on the Universe.* Richmond Hill, Ontario: Firefly Books, 2003.

———. *Uranus, Neptune, and Pluto.* Minneapolis: Lerner Books, 2000.

Miller, Ron. *Uranus and Neptune.* Brookfield, Conn.: Twenty-First Century Books, 2003.

Sagan, Carl. *Pale Blue Dot: A Vision of the Human Future in Space.* New York: Random House, 1994.

Stille, Darlene. *Uranus.* Chanhassen, Minn.: Child's World, 2004.

Tocci, Salvatore. *A Look at Uranus.* New York: Franklin Watts, 2003.